THE DOPAMINE TRIAGE

The Protocol to Reclaim Focus in an Algorithm-Driven World

Marcus Thorne

The Cognitive Control Series, Book 1

First Edition

ISBN: 978-93-5773-118-8

Cover design by Marcus Thorne

Interior layout by Marcus Thorne

Contents

INTRODUCTION

The Phantom Buzz

You are trying to focus on a particular task in a quiet room, suddenly feeling the unmistakable vibration against your leg. A quick jolt runs through you before you even notice it. To reflex it you pull out the device from your pocket and look at its blank screen, and found no new notification on screen, nothing happens around you.

I want you to know you're not making this up. It's not in your head. Your nervous system has basically been forced to rewire itself just to keep up with the constant noise and pressure you're under every day. It is trying to adapt to a new environment where it treats every digital input as top priority.

We have already created a false equivalence between our real requirements and device notification. We feel same tactile when we see a casual message, a social media update, and a critical family update. **The device doesn't have the ability to differentiate the severity of the inputs;** your brain is always waiting for the next thing to happen.

When this happens, know that it's not your fault. It's not just a lack of discipline or a weakness on your part; the entire setup is broken. The situation is such that as soon as a paramedic hears the sound of the pager, your body is accustomed to respond to the vibration or notification of the phone in your pocket. It's a kind of unrealistic emergency that keeps haunting you all the time.

As soon as the phone rings, it seems like something very important, because our lifestyle or technology has not yet reached a level that will teach our nervous system to be a little calmer. We have not made any rules or system for ourselves that will get us out of this turmoil.

Systemic Overload

Don't beat yourself up for not being able to focus. When your nerves are this frayed, your judgment naturally gets a bit hazy. It's almost impossible not to make a mistake when you're feeling that unsettled.

This isn't a glitch in your biology or a failure of your body. It's just that you're dealing with a systemic overload.

The apps we scroll through every day aren't built to help us and then let us go. They're actually designed to keep us hooked. They don't have a 'stop' button or a way to say, 'Okay, you've had enough.' Instead, they just keep feeding us more, making it almost impossible to just put the phone down.

The way these apps are built just floods us with noise. Every time you swipe or refresh, it hits you with something new. The problem is, the system doesn't care if it's a life-changing message or just a random notification, it just keeps piling everything on top of you at once.

When the world is built to keep you constantly buzzing, losing your focus isn't a personal failure. Your brain is just trying to survive a landslide of data. You haven't lost your depth; you're just standing in a room where everyone is screaming at the top of their lungs, and you're exhausted from trying to hear the one voice that actually matters.

The Triage Protocol

It's exhausting to feel like you're in a constant tug-of-war with your phone. When every buzz and headline is designed to scream for your attention, sheer willpower just isn't enough to win. Fighting the device or hiding from it for a weekend is just a temporary fix. What we actually need is a way to live with this technology without letting it run our lives.

It requires the Triage Protocol.

Think about doctors in an ER. They don't run to whoever is screaming the loudest; they stay calm and use 'triage' to decide what actually needs their help first.

Our digital lives need that same calm. We have to stop treating every flash on our phone like a call to emergency services.

By setting up your own 'triage' system, you build a protective wall around your mind. You learn to listen for the signals that actually matter, and let the rest of the noise just fade into the background.

The Promise

I am not writing another list of productivity hacks. I have no interest in teaching you how to answer emails faster. And I am certainly not asking you to abandon the digital world and live in a cabin. I am writing this to give you a redesign, a fundamental architectural shift in how you relate to information.

Through this protocol, you'll create a sterile field around your mind, a space where noise no longer dictates your attention. You won't rely on willpower alone. You'll build a system that decides what deserves access.

Your focus will become protected territory. The trivial fades. The essential remains.

This isn't about escaping modern life. It's about standing inside it without being pushed around.

PHASE 1: THE STERILE FIELD

CHAPTER 1: SANITIZING THE WORKSPACE

The Sterile Field

Think about an operating room for a second. Before a surgeon even touches a patient, the room has to be perfect. It's scrubbed down, the tools are laid out in a specific order, and there's absolutely zero clutter. Why? Because you'd never trust a doctor to perform a delicate, life-saving surgery in a messy room full of trash. We know that chaos leads to mistakes and infections.

Yet, this is exactly what we expect of our own minds every single day.

But look at how we treat ourselves. Whenever we sit down for something important and open our laptops, we're met with a screen buried under messy files and random screenshots. Our browsers are even worse, clogged with twenty tabs from three days ago that look like they're suffocating. Then there's our phones, packed with colourful apps we never use and a sea of red notifications. We sit right in the middle of this digital landfill and somehow expect our minds to stay calm and do deep, focused work.

To understand why this mess destroys our focus, we have to look at how the brain actually handles what it sees. Our eyes aren't just passive cameras taking snapshots; they are active processors. When your screen is buried under a mountain of clutter, your brain can't just "ignore" it. It actually burns through your mental energy just trying to filter that junk out. Every single old file sitting on your desktop acts as a "micro-reminder", a tiny nudge about an unfinished task, a project you abandoned, or an email you still haven't sent. Simply put, visual chaos leads to mental fog.

This is especially true for open browser tabs. In psychology, every open tab acts like an 'open loop', a thought you started but never quite finished. You might be focused on writing a document right now, but your subconscious is still 'watching' those other tabs. Because of this, those unfinished thoughts keep humming in the back of your mind, quietly draining your mental energy without you even realizing it.

I believe relying on willpower alone to stay focused is a losing game. Our willpower isn't an infinite resource; it's more like a battery that slowly drains as the day goes on. At the end of the day, how we behave is shaped by the environment we're in. So, before diving into the chaos of digital noise, we have to prep our space. Just like a surgeon wouldn't start without a clean room, we need to 'sterilize' our digital workspace before we ever try to do our best work.

The Mechanism

Why Your Brain Can't Ignore the Mess

You think you aren't looking at them.

You have convinced yourself that the forty-seven icons scattered across your desktop are just "background." You believe that because you aren't actively clicking on them, they aren't costing you anything.

But you are wrong.

Your brain does not have a "minimizing" feature. It doesn't work like a browser window.

Your visual system is highly sensitive to contrast and change. It is constantly, relentlessly scanning your environment for changes, for tools, for danger, for food. It processes everything in your peripheral vision, whether you want it to or not.

Every single icon on that screen is a jagged edge.

When you sit down to write a report, and there is a PDF of a contract sitting three inches to the right of your document, your brain has to expend a tiny, imperceptible amount of energy to suppress it. It has to say, *"Not that. Not that. Not that. Focus on the Word doc."*

It does this ten times a second.

It is a low-grade, background hum of inhibition.

Engineers call this "cognitive load." I call it a leak.

You are bleeding processing power before you even type a sentence.

This is why you feel tired at 10:00 AM. You haven't done any hard work yet. But you have spent two hours fighting your own wallpaper. You have forced your brain to filter out a hundred competing signals just to find the one signal that matters.

And then there is the emotional weight.

Those icons aren't just pixels. They are open loops.

That screenshot you took three weeks ago? That's a decision you delayed. That "Read Later" folder? That's a guilt trip. That half-finished spreadsheet? That's a deadline screaming at you in a whisper.

When you leave these things visible, you are surrounding yourself with unfinished business. You are trying to work in a room where everyone is tapping you on the shoulder.

You might have "tuned it out." But your subconscious hasn't. It is keeping a tally of every promise you made to yourself and broke.

It creates background tension. It makes you want to tab away. It makes you want to check your phone. It makes you want to leave the desk.

We often blame our lack of focus on "discipline." We think we are just lazy.

But it's rarely a discipline problem. It's an environment problem.

If you put a recovering alcoholic in a bar, you don't blame them for looking at the bottles. If you put a knowledge worker in a digital junkyard, you shouldn't blame them for feeling scattered.

The brain seeks order. If it can't find it in the environment, it has to build it internally. That costs energy. Expensive energy.

Stop asking your brain to be a janitor.

Let it be an architect.

Clear the floor so it can build.

The Resistance

"But I Need to See It to Remember It"

I know what you are thinking.

You are looking at the mess, and you feel a tightness in your chest. You are afraid to delete it. You are afraid to even hide it.

"If I file this away," you tell yourself, *"I will forget it exists."*

This is the most common lie in the digital world.

We have conflated "visibility" with "memory." We treat our desktop like a bulletin board, pinning up every task, every invoice, and every idea, assuming that if we stare at it long enough, we will eventually do it.

Be honest.

How long has that PDF been sitting in the top right corner? Three weeks? Two months?

If seeing it was going to make you do it, you would have done it by now.

The truth is, leaving it on the desktop actually makes you *less* likely to do it. It's the "Banner Blindness" effect. When you see an advertisement on a website every single day, your brain eventually learns to edit it out completely. You literally stop seeing it.

The same thing happens to your files. They stop being tasks and start being texture. They become part of the furniture.

The fear of "out of sight, out of mind" is valid, but the solution isn't clutter. The solution is a system.

You are afraid that if you put the file in a folder, it dies. That is because you don't trust your own retrieval process. You don't trust yourself to check the folder.

So, you resort to "Hoarding by Default."

You keep everything on the surface, just in case. It feels safer. It feels like you are in control.

But look at the cost.

You are trading clarity for a false sense of security. You are terrifying your present self to comfort your future self.

And the irony? You are losing things anyway.

When everything is important, nothing is important. When your desktop is a sea of 200 icons, you can't find the one you need. You spend five minutes searching for the file that is staring you in the face.

That isn't a system. That is a scavenger hunt.

You have to let go of the idea that your desktop is a storage unit. It is not.

It is a workbench.

If you were a carpenter, you wouldn't pile every piece of wood, every saw, every hammer, and every receipt for the last ten years onto your workbench. You wouldn't have room to cut a straight line.

You would hang the tools on the wall. You would put the wood in the rack. You would keep the surface clean.

Not because you are "neat." But because you have work to do.

Don't let the fear of forgetting paralyze you. If a task is important, it belongs on a calendar or a to-do list. It does not belong on your wallpaper.

Move it.

The Toolkit

The Nuclear Option & The Holding Tank

We are not going to organize your desktop.

"Organizing" is a trap. It takes hours. You will open a folder, start reading old files, get distracted, and three hours later, you will have moved six icons.

We don't have time for that.

We are going to use the Nuclear Option.

This takes exactly sixty seconds.

Step 1: The One-Folder Rule Create a single archive folder and move everything into it in one sweep. "OLD_DESKTOP_[Today's Date]".

Step 2: The Sweep Select every single icon on your screen. All of them. The screenshots, the folders, the apps, the loose files. Drag them into that new folder.

Step 3: The Breath Look at your screen.

It is empty.

Do not panic. Nothing is deleted. Nothing is lost. It is all sitting safely in that folder, exactly one click away. If you need something, you can go get it.

But for now, the visual noise is gone.

Step 4: The Wallpaper Reset Most people have a photo of their kids, or a landscape, or a "motivational quote" as their background. These are high-contrast images. They hide icons. They create camouflage. Change it. Set your background to a solid, neutral colour. Grey. Muted Blue. Black.

Make the background boring. The work should be the only interesting thing on the screen.

The Maintenance: The "Holding Tank" Protocol

Now that you are at zero, files will try to creep back in. You will download a PDF. You will save a screenshot.

That is fine. But they cannot stay there.

Create one folder in the center of your screen called "INBOX" or "HOLDING TANK."

This is the only place files are allowed to live temporarily.

- Downloaded a receipt? Put it in the Tank.
- Working on a presentation? Keep the shortcut in the Tank.

The Rule: The Tank must be emptied every Friday. (We will cover this in the Hygiene chapter).

But for the rest of the week, the rest of the screen is sacred ground.

If you catch yourself saving a file to the desktop, stop. Drag it to the Tank.

Protect the sterile field.

Strategic Reminder

A clean desktop does not make you smarter. It does not make you faster. But it removes the friction that makes you slow. It stops the leak. You are plugging the holes in the bucket before you try to fill it with water.

Action 1: The Zero-Icon Desktop Policy

Let's take a look at your screen, what's the first thing you see? Most of us treat our digital desktop like a quick 'holding area' for files. But over time, it turns into a massive pile of downloaded PDFs, random screenshots, and icons for apps we barely use. We start out thinking of it as a temporary workspace, but it quickly shifts into a permanent graveyard for unfinished projects.

Every icon on your screen is essentially a 'trigger.' In the world of behavioural psychology, these are environmental cues that nudge your subconscious into certain habits or trains of thought. Imagine you're deep in the zone, working on an urgent proposal, when your eyes happen to graze over your inbox icon, a web browser, or a folder labeled 'Taxes.' Even if you don't click on them, your brain has already registered those options. They create a tiny mental stir, pulling a piece of your attention away from what actually matters.

You're essentially forcing yourself to fight the urge to click those icons. Even before you've properly started your real work, you've already burned through a chunk of your mental energy just trying to tune out the mess around you.

Establishing your sterile area starts with a single, non-negotiable rule: the zero-icon desktop policy. It is exactly as literal as it sounds. Your computer screen should be a total blank slate, no scattered files, no cluttered folders, and zero app shortcuts. Just a wide-open, clean background.

The logic is simple, but it completely flips the way you work. When your desktop is empty, your computer loses its power to distract you. You stop being reactive, no longer jumping at whatever file or shortcut happens to be staring you in the face.

Instead, you're forced to start with a clear, specific goal, moving only toward what you actually intended to do.

Without icons to click on, you're forced to actually use the search bar to find what you need. That tiny, conscious hurdle is exactly what makes this work. It breaks that "auto-pilot" loop in your brain and forces you to pause and ask yourself: "Wait, what exactly am I here to do right now?

Implementing this doesn't require hours of tedious sorting. You don't need to perfectly organize years of digital clutter right this second.

Just do one simple thing: create a new folder on your main drive and name it "Archive" or "To Sort." Select every single file and folder currently on your desktop and drop them into that one folder. That's it! If you want an even faster fix, both Windows and Mac have settings that let you "hide" all desktop icons with just one click.

The sense of instant relief is undeniable. When you open your laptop tomorrow morning, you won't be hit by a wall of demands or a messy pile of unfinished tasks. Instead, you'll be greeted by a quiet, open space, a sterile field perfectly prepared for your best thinking.

Action 2: Single-Purpose Device Mode

Think about any high-stakes workplace, every tool has one specific job. In an emergency ward, a monitor is there strictly to track a patient's vitals; no one would ever use it to catch up on a movie. You'd never see a sterile surgical tray being used to hold a doctor's lunch. In those environments, tools have a single, non-negotiable purpose.

To understand why this is such a big problem for your focus, we have to look at a mental process called "associative activation." Your brain is essentially a prediction engine. It looks at your surroundings to decide what "mode" it should be in and how much energy it should spend. For example, when you sit upright at a desk, your brain takes that as a cue to start gearing up for work. But the moment you stretch out on a sofa, your brain starts receiving signals to power down and rest.

But when your main device becomes a universal portal for both high-pressure work and mindless entertainment, those mental boundaries just collapse. Your brain no longer knows which "mode" it's supposed to be in the moment you open the screen.

Because that one device represents both intense deadlines and an easy escape, your mind tries to hold onto both states at the same time. Even when you're just trying to kick back and watch a video, the "architecture" of your office is only one click away. This keeps your nervous system in a state of low-level alert, a quiet, chronic fatigue known as context-switching stress.

The solution is to move toward a "Single-Purpose Device" mindset. It's about being intentional and physically separating our digital tools based on what we actually use them for.

If you have the means, draw a hard physical line between your lives. Use your work computer strictly for work, and keep a separate tablet or laptop for your downtime, like watching movies or chatting. When the workday is done, don't just shut the device down, hide it. Put it in a drawer or another room so it's physically out of sight. At that point, it's officially off-limits.

If you can't use separate devices, you have to build a digital wall instead. Set up two completely different user profiles on your computer: one for "Work" and one for "Personal."

Your work profile should be a distraction-free zone, no personal messaging apps, no games, and definitely no streaming bookmarks. On the flip side, keep your personal profile for yourself; don't even log into your work email or project tools there.

This step isn't about sucking the joy out of your life; it's about protecting your headspace. By splitting up your digital world, you're giving your brain permission to go "all in" when it's time to work, and to completely shut down when it's time to rest. You're being intentional about saving your energy, making sure that when you finally step away from the noise, you can actually recover.

CHAPTER 2: THE NOTIFICATION FIREWALL

Your Attention is a Secure Facility

Think of a high-security environment, like a sterile operating room, an air traffic control tower, or a top-secret lab. Access to these places is strictly guarded. You don't just wander in to have a chat. There are checkpoints. There are protocols. There are doors that won't open unless you have the right level of clearance.

These security measures aren't there because the people inside are being secretive or unfriendly. It's because the work they are doing is important. To keep that work precise and high-quality, they have to protect their space from any kind of outside "pollution" or distraction.

Your mind is no different. Your attention is a finite, high-value resource, it is the only tool you have to navigate the world, make big decisions, and connect with the people you love. By its very nature, your focus should be a 'secured facility.

Yet, most of us live our digital lives with a 'broken door' policy.

The state of our digital world is such that we give a 'breaking news' alert from another continent the same priority as an urgent call from a family member. We let a discount coupon from a food app vibrate in our pockets with the same intensity as an emergency text from our boss. Put simply, we've completely lost the ability to distinguish what actually matters from what doesn't.

When everything is treated as 'urgent,' nothing actually is. This leaves us in a constant, jittery state of reactive panic. You aren't just 'distracted'; your mental space is being invaded.

To regain control of your attention, you need to set up a "notification firewall." This isn't about cutting yourself off from the rest of the world; it's about checking everyone's credentials at the door. Before anything is allowed to interrupt you, you should ask one simple, powerful question: *"Who actually has the badge to get in?"*

The Mechanism

The Slot Machine in Your Pocket

You think you check your phone to get information. You think you are looking for a specific email, or a text from your spouse, or the weather forecast.

You aren't.

If you were just checking for data, you would do it on a schedule. You would check at 9:00 AM, get the data, and stop.

But you don't do that. You check when you are bored. You check when you are anxious. You check when you are standing in an elevator for four seconds.

You are not looking for information. You are looking for a reward.

The mechanism driving this behaviour is precise. It is the same psychological engine that keeps a gambler sitting at a slot machine for twelve hours without eating.

It is called Intermittent Reinforcement.

Here is how the trap works:

If you pulled the lever on a slot machine and it gave you a dollar every single time, you would get bored. It's predictable. There is no thrill. If you pulled the lever and it *never* gave you a dollar, you would quit. It's useless.

But if the machine gives you a dollar *sometimes*, randomly, unpredictably, with no pattern you can figure out, you will keep pulling longer than you intended.

The uncertainty is the drug.

Your phone is the most efficient slot machine ever built.

Every time you hear a *ding* or feel a buzz, the machine is spinning. You don't know what it is. It might be a boring email from HR (a loss). It might be a spam text (a loss). Or, it might be a message from a friend, a "like" on your photo, or a breaking news alert that confirms your worldview (a win).

You don't check the notification to see the content. You check to relieve the tension of *not knowing.*

The engineers who designed these systems understand this biology better than you do. They know that if they can trigger the "seeking" circuit in your brain, they capture your attention.

That is why the refresh interaction is designed the way it is. Notice the "pull-to-refresh" motion on your feed. You drag down, the wheel spins (tension), and then *pop*, new content appears (reward). It is physically identical to pulling a lever.

And then there is the Red Badge.

Why are notification bubbles red? They could be blue. They could be green. But they are red because Red is a signal colour. It cuts through visual noise faster than almost any other colour.

Your visual cortex is Highly sensitive to prioritize red above all other colours. It signals danger. It demands immediate attention. When you see a red dot on an app icon, your brain registers it as an "unfinished task" or a "threat."

It creates a microscopic itch. *Something is wrong. Something needs to be cleared.*

You tap the app not to enjoy the content, but just to get rid of the dot. You are cleaning up the threat.

This is why "willpower" doesn't work against notifications. You are fighting a reflex the system relies on to resolve uncertainty and neutralize threats.

As long as the phone is buzzing, part of your attention remains on standby. It cannot focus on deep work because it is waiting for the next spin of the wheel.

You aren't weak. You are just being played by a system that hacked your hardware.

To win, you have to stop playing. You have to rig the machine so it stops spinning.

The Resistance

"But What If Someone Needs Me?"

This is the hardest part.

Turning off notifications is technically easy. It takes three clicks in the settings menu. The hard part is the silence that follows.

For the first twenty-four hours, you will feel a phantom anxiety. You will look at your dark screen and think, *"I am missing something."*

You will convince yourself that the world is burning down and you are the only one with the fire extinguisher.

"What if my boss emails me about the deadline?" "What if my partner needs me to pick up milk?" "What if there is a crisis?"

Let's dismantle this fear. It is usually a lie.

The Emergency Myth We have conflated "information" with "emergency." A text message from a friend is information. A sale on sneakers is information. A slack message about a meeting next Tuesday is information. None of these are emergencies.

An emergency is blood, fire, or immediate financial collapse.

If your child breaks their arm at school, the school will not email you. They will not send a push notification to your wrist. They will call you. Repeatedly.

That is why the VIP Protocol (which allows phone calls from key contacts to bypass Do Not Disturb) works. It filters out the *noise* while guaranteeing the *signal.*

If your phone isn't ringing, the building isn't burning.

The "Responsiveness" Trap The deeper fear isn't about safety. It's about status.

You are afraid that if you don't reply instantly, people will think you are lazy. You worry that your value as an employee or a friend is tied to your speed.

"I'm the guy who is always on top of things," you tell yourself.

Be careful. You are confusing "responsiveness" with "reliability."

If you reply to every email within thirty seconds, you have not proven that you are a hard worker. You have proven that you have no priorities. You have proven that your time has zero defensive value.

You have trained your colleagues to treat you like a vending machine: they push a button, and you dispense an answer.

You taught them to interrupt you.

When you install the Firewall, you are retraining them. You are changing the terms of engagement.

Yes, there will be friction. Your boss might ask, *"Did you see my message?"* Your partner might say, *"Why didn't you text me back?"*

This is the moment of resistance. Do not apologize. If you apologize, you are admitting you did something wrong. You didn't. You were working.

The Script: *"I was in a deep work block for the last two hours. I'm seeing your message now. What do you need?"*

Say it without guilt. You are trading "instant availability" for "focused execution."

Most reasonable people respect that trade. In fact, they usually envy it. They know, deep down, that the person who is always online is the person who isn't getting the real work done.

Respect is not given to the fastest responder. It is given to the person who delivers the result.

The silence isn't empty. It's heavy. It's the weight of you actually doing your job.

Strategic Reminder

Responsiveness is a cheap metric. It is easy to measure, so we obsess over it. Impact is hard to measure, so we ignore it. Don't let the easy metric kill the hard one.

The Toolkit

The Three-Tier Security Protocol

We are not just "turning off notifications." That is too blunt. If you turn off everything, you will eventually panic and turn everything back on.

We are building a Tiered Access System.

Think of your phone like a government building.

- Tier 1: The Oval Office. (Immediate, unrestricted access).
- Tier 2: The Press Room. (Scheduled briefings only).
- Tier 3: The Street. (No access).

You need to assign every single app on your phone to one of these tiers. Right now.

Tier 1: The VIPs (Immediate Access) These are the people whose calls you *must* answer. Not "want to," but *must*.

- Who: Spouse, School Nurse, Boss (optional), Elderly Parents.
- The setting: Use "Emergency Bypass" or "Focus Mode Exceptions."

> Use your device's "Emergency Bypass" or equivalent setting to allow specific contacts to break through Do Not Disturb.

- The Result: Your phone is silent 24/7. But if *these specific people* call, it rings loud and clear. They have the red phone.

Tier 2: The Batch (Scheduled Summary) This is for human communication that is not an emergency.

- o Who: WhatsApp groups, Slack (unless you are on-call), Email, SMS from friends.
- o The setting: Do not let these buzz. But do not hide them forever.

    Use "Scheduled Summary" (iOS) or a batched notification app (Android).

    Set delivery for 8:00 AM, 12:00 PM, and 5:00 PM.

- o The Result: You don't see the message when *they* send it. You see it when *you* are ready. You are moving from "Real-Time" to "Asynchronous."

Tier 3: The Noise (Hard Block) This is for machines.

- o Who: News, Social Media, Games, Uber Eats, Shopping, Netflix.
- o The setting: Switch to a neutral, low-contrast background.
- o Crucial Step: Turn off the Badges (the red dots).

    Even if the phone doesn't buzz, a screen full of red dots is a visual scream. It triggers the same cortisol spike.

    Turn off "Badges" for Mail, Slack, and Social.

    If you don't see the dot, you won't feel the itch.

The "Peace of Mind" Script

The biggest reason people fail to implement the Firewall is social guilt. They are afraid their partner will get mad if they don't reply instantly.

You have to explain the protocol *before* you start it. You are not ignoring them; you are prioritizing them.

Send this text to your VIPs (Spouse/Partner):

"Hey, I'm trying a new focus workflow to get less distracted. My phone is going to be on silent most of the day so I can actually work.

But I have set you as a VIP.

If you call, it will always ring through. If you text, I might not see it for a few hours. If it's urgent, please call. You are the only one with this access."

Send this to your Team (if you are brave):

"I am checking email at 10am, 2pm, and 4pm to focus on [Project X]. If this is a true emergency, call my cell. Otherwise, I'll clear the inbox during those blocks."

Most people won't be annoyed. They will be impressed. You are signalling that your time is scarce, which automatically makes it more valuable.

The Hard Reset Option If you still find yourself checking the phone just to "look," it is because you are addicted to the palette, not the information.

Silicon Valley engineers use saturated colors—specifically bright red, to trigger your amygdala. It is the same visual psychology used in slot machines. The color itself is a reward signal.

Strip the stimulus.

Locate the "Color Filters" or "Grayscale" mode buried in your device's Accessibility settings. Turn it on and leave it on.

Without colour, Instagram looks like a surveillance feed. Candy Crush looks like a spreadsheet. The visual stimulation drops dramatically.

Use this when you are weak. It makes the device boring. And boring is safe.

Strategic Reminder You are not missing out. The fear that you are missing "breaking news" or a "viral moment" is a hallucination. If it's important, the world will find a way to tell you. If it's not, you just saved yourself five minutes of your life. Keep the door locked.

Action 1: The VIP Protocol

Think of the triage nurse at a hospital's front desk. Their job isn't just to be polite; their real responsibility is to discriminate between cases.

They have to decide in a split second: who has a minor sprain and who is having a heart attack? If they were 'kind' enough to let everyone through to the doctors at once, the whole system would collapse. The people who actually needed life-saving care would be the ones who pay the price.

The problem with your phone is that it has no sense of priority. By default, it treats a casual 'hello' from an old acquaintance with the exact same urgency as an emergency call from your spouse. It's as if you've handed out a key to the front door of your mind to every single person you've ever met.

To protect your focus, you have to step in and act as your own 'manual triage nurse.' It's time to launch what I call the 'VIP Protocol.

To pull this off, you'll need to dive into your phone's "Emergency Bypass" or "Exception" settings, you can usually find these hidden inside Do Not Disturb or Focus mode. You are essentially hand-picking a "whitelist" of your loved ones or anyone who truly matters, ensuring their calls and messages cut through the silence to reach you, no matter what's happening in the digital world.

Defining the Criteria

The biggest mistake people make here is letting their emotions take over. They end up adding their best friends, their entire extended family, and every favorite coworker just because they're afraid of being rude or 'unreachable.' But doing that completely defeats the point of the protocol.

Your VIP list isn't a scorecard for how much you love someone. It's a purely practical decision: whose call or message is so critical that it justifies interrupting your deep work right now?

You need to ask yourself one simple, high-stakes question: '*Who is actually likely to give me news so urgent that I'd need to drop everything and run right this second?*"

To help you prune your list, here is a breakdown of who actually deserves a "key" to your focus and why:

- Your Spouse or Partner: Yes. They are your primary emergency contact. If the house is on fire or a pipe burst, you need to know.
- Your Child's School or Caretaker: Yes. If your child gets hurt or sick, this is a non-negotiable interruption. You need to be reachable instantly.
- Your Direct Manager: Yes, but with a catch. If your job involves high-stakes crises (like IT outages or PR fires), they need access. However, if you are a knowledge worker who needs deep focus, try a "calls-only" rule. Let them call you if it's a true emergency, but keep their emails and Slack messages silent until you're ready.
- Your Elderly Parents: Yes. For medical emergencies, they belong on the list.
- Your Best Friend: Probably not. A funny meme sent at 2:00 PM is not an emergency; it's just conversation. It can wait until you've finished your deep work and are ready to relax.

The Psychology of Silence

The real magic of the VIP Protocol isn't just that it shuts out the world; it's that it quiets the noise inside your own head.

Most of us are stuck in a loop of 'ghost checking' our phones, scrolling just in case something happened. We live in a constant state of FOMO, afraid we'll miss that one life-changing alert. But once you strictly define your VIPs, that anxiety simply vanishes. You can breathe again because you know, with absolute certainty, that if a real crisis hits, your phone will make noise.

This certainty acts like a mental safety net. It gives you the permission to ignore your device for hours, resting in the confidence that silence is a sign of safety. If your phone is quiet, it means your world is okay. And in that silence, you finally have the freedom to do your best work.

Action 2: Hard-Blocking Non-Human Inputs

Once you've drawn a clear line for the people in your life, it's time to take a hard look at your devices.

If you take a look back at the notifications you received over the last week, you'll probably notice something interesting: most of them didn't come from a real person. They came from a server. They were just automated scripts, pre-programmed nudges specifically designed to bait you back into an app.

A 'breaking news' alert about some distant political scandal. A notification that a complete stranger 'liked' your photo. A reminder from a game that your daily reward is ready. A nudge from a shopping app about a flash sale.

These aren't messages. They aren't people reaching out. They are just hooks designed to reel you back in.

If you look at it through the lens of a medical triage model, these notifications are the equivalent of a hospital administrator bursting into the emergency room every five minutes to scream about 'today's special in the cafeteria.' It's just noise disguised as a message. Simply put, it's a calculated attempt to hijack your brain's 'critical care', your ability to focus deeply on what matters.

To clean up your digital world, you need to follow one simple, non-negotiable rule*: If a flesh-and-blood human didn't personally type that message to you, it doesn't deserve your attention."*

The Protocol:

To protect your focus, you have to strip every non-human or automated source of its 'all-access pass' to your brain. This requires you to go into your settings and do a one-time, top-to-bottom sweep of every single app.

Silence these apps now to protect your attention:

- o News Apps: Turn off all push notifications immediately. News should be something you seek out when you need it; it shouldn't be a 'panic signal' causing unnecessary vibrations in your pocket. Remember, 'breaking news' is often designed to trigger cortisol spikes rather than simply inform you. If there's a real emergency, like a natural disaster, a government alert or your VIPs will reach you.

- o Social media: Kill notifications for likes, comments, tags, or friend suggestions. These are essentially dopamine traps engineered to keep you checking your phone. If you want to see who liked your post, do it on your own terms. Don't let the app demand your time.

- Games and Entertainment: Mute every game, streaming service, and delivery app. These platforms use notifications strictly for retention. They are harvesting your most valuable asset, your focus, just to boost their business metrics.

By shutting down these automated alerts, you aren't 'missing out' on the world. You are simply closing a security breach. You are ensuring that whenever your phone actually makes a sound, it represents a real human connection, a heartbeat from your inner circle, rather than a hollow 'ping' from a cold database.

PHASE 2: THE TRIAGE PROTOCOL

CHAPTER 3: CODE GREEN, THE NOISE

You've done it. We all have.

You pick up your phone for one specific thing, maybe to check the weather or send a quick reply, and twenty minutes later, you suddenly 'wake up.' You've spiraled deep into vacation photos from someone you barely know. You've watched six straight videos of someone restoring a rusty knife. You don't even remember clicking on them.

The screen is glowing. The content is moving. But if you check your pulse, you'll see it's perfectly calm.

This isn't focus. It isn't being 'busy.' It's a trance.

In emergency medicine, the "Green" triage category is specifically reserved for the "walking wounded", patients with minor injuries like small cuts, bruises, or sprains. While their injuries are real, they are not life-threatening and do not require immediate surgical or trauma care.

The danger isn't the minor injury. It's what happens when too many of them show up at once, if these low-priority cases are allowed to flood the emergency room without a triage filter, they consume the critical resources, time, space, and attention, needed to save patients facing "Red" priority emergencies, such as a heart attack.

In your digital life, Code Green is just noise. It's the infinite scroll, the vast, churning ocean of content that asks nothing of you and gives nothing back.

We like to call this "relaxing."

But it really isn't. It's just numbing.

There is a predictable psychological reason why staring at a screen for an hour can leave you feeling more exhausted than when you started. It comes down to the fundamental difference between satisfaction and relief.

The engineers in Silicon Valley understand this psychology far better than we do. They didn't build these feeds to be helpful; they built them to be bottomless.

Every time you swipe down to 'refresh' an app, you're essentially pulling the lever of a digital slot machine. You might get an annoying work email (a loss), or you might find a shocking headline or a funny video (a win). It's that constant uncertainty, the 'What will I get next?' that keeps you hooked. It's the unpredictability that makes it so hard to look away.

This creates a cycle of "cheap dopamine." It requires zero effort from you. You haven't solved a single problem, finished a project, or even truly connected with a friend. All you've done is flick your thumb.

Cheap dopamine feels good for exactly three seconds. Then it evaporates, leaving behind a void that demands to be filled again. Immediately.

Most of us didn't even notice when the shift happened. We stopped using these devices as tools and started treating them like a feeding habit. We've traded the deep, slow satisfaction of actually doing something for the quick, low-quality buzz of just watching things.

And just like an emergency waiting room overflowing with minor injuries, this noise is suffocating the real work of your life. It's time to clear the corridors.

The Mechanism

The Bottomless Bowl

You think you lack self-control. You think you are scrolling because you are interested in the content.

You aren't.

You are scrolling because the engineers removed the brakes.

Ten years ago, the internet had edges. When you reached the bottom of a webpage or a search result, you hit a hard stop. To see more, you had to find a button that said "Next Page" or "Load More."

You had to click.

That click was a Stopping Cue.

It was a tiny moment of friction. It forced your brain to make a conscious decision: *"Do I want to spend more time on this? Is it worth the effort?"*

That millisecond of choice was enough to wake you up. It was an exit ramp.

But the platforms realized something: every time you hit a stopping cue, you had a chance to leave. And usually, you did.

So they removed the stopping cues.

They invented the Infinite Scroll.

Now, when your thumb reaches the bottom of the screen, the app automatically loads the next piece of content before you even realize you've finished the last one.

There is no "Next" button. There is no friction. There is no decision point.

The default behaviour shifted from *"Click to continue"* to *"Scroll to stop."*

This change is profound. Before, you had to actively choose to consume. Now, you have to actively choose to stop consuming.

And human beings are terrible at stopping.

We tend to finish what is placed in front of us. If you give a person a plate of food, they will eat until the plate is empty, not until they are full. They rely on the visual cue of the empty plate to tell them, *"You are done."*

There was a famous experiment where researchers gave people a "bottomless soup bowl", a bowl that secretly refilled itself from the bottom as they ate. People didn't stop. They ate 73% more soup than normal. They ate until they felt sick. Why? Because the bowl never got empty. Their eyes never saw the stopping cue.

Your feed is the bottomless soup bowl.

It is designed to be unfinishable.

You scroll for an hour not because you are finding valuable information, but because your brain is waiting for the "end" signal. It is waiting for the empty plate.

But the plate never empties. The content just keeps loading.

This is why you feel that specific, hollow exhaustion after a long session on social media. You aren't satisfied. You've consumed beyond your natural stopping point. You have consumed way past the point of satiety, simply because the mechanism didn't give you a polite way to leave.

You aren't addicted to the content. Most of it is garbage. You are trapped in a design pattern that removed the exit signs.

To escape, you can't rely on your intuition to tell you when you're done. Your intuition is broken by the design. You have to build your own "Next Page" button. You have to artificially insert the stopping cue that they took away.

The Resistance

The Fear of Irrelevance

The primary friction in reducing noise is not boredom. It is the fear of losing social currency.

We consume low-value information, news snippets, memes, trending topics, because we view them as the language of connection. We worry that if we disconnect from the stream, we will have nothing to say. We fear becoming "the person who doesn't know."

This is a valid status calculation. In many circles, being "plugged in" is a proxy for being sharp.

However, we must distinguish between Signal and Noise.

- Signal is information that changes your decisions or understanding of the world.
- Noise is data that merely updates you on the current state of chaos.

Most "breaking news" is Noise. It is ephemeral. It is relevant at 9:00 AM and obsolete by 4:00 PM. Spending memory on it is rarely worth the cost.

The Resistance argues: *"But I need to be informed to be a responsible citizen/professional."*

Analysis: There is a difference between being Informed and being Current.

Being *Current* requires constant, low-latency monitoring of a feed. It is a full-time job with zero output. Being *Informed* requires deep consumption of synthesized analysis, usually days or weeks after the event, when the facts are verified.

When you step out of the stream, you do not become ignorant. You become selective.

You will miss the meme. You will miss the outrage of the morning.

But in exchange, you regain the capacity for synthesis. You stop trading in the low-value currency of "what just happened" and start trading in the high-value currency of "what it means."

The initial feeling of isolation is not a defect. It is the system recalibrating from reactive processing to reflective thought.

The Toolkit

Architecture of Friction

We cannot rely on willpower to resist the infinite scroll. Willpower is a finite resource; the feed is infinite. The only viable defence is Friction.

We must architect the environment so that accessing "Noise" requires high effort, while accessing "Work" requires low effort. We invert the current default.

The Device Separation Protocol

The smartphone is a convergence device. It combines the tool (email, maps, notes) with the toy (social, news, games). This convergence is the root of the distraction.

The strategy is Functional Divergence.

- The Phone is a Utility: It is for logistics, maps, and communication.
- The Desktop is for Work: It is for creation and deep processing.
- The Tablet (or specialized device) is for Consumption: It is for reading and watching.

The Rule: Consider removing all "Infinite Scroll" applications from the utility device (Phone). If an application has no "stopping cue" (Twitter, Instagram, TikTok, News Aggregators), it does not belong in your pocket.

It belongs on a stationary device.

If you want to check the feed, you must physically move to a different context. You must sit at a computer or pick up a tablet.

This introduces Physical Friction. The urge to "just check" usually cannot survive the requirement to stand up and walk to another room.

The Browser Barrier

If you must access these platforms on your phone, use the browser, not the App.

Applications are engineered for fluidity. They preload content to ensure zero latency. They are frictionless. Mobile websites are clunky. They require logins. They load slower. The interface is often inferior.

This inferiority is a feature, not a bug.

Force yourself to log in every time. Do not save the password. Those ten seconds are often enough to interrupt the impulse. and ask: *"Is this worth it?"*

Grayscale as a De-Stimulant

Colour is a data point used by the brain to assess value. Bright, saturated colours signal "reward." By rendering the display in Grayscale, you strip the visual data of its emotional valence. The content remains readable, but the visual stimulation drops significantly.

Use this not as a punishment, but as a filter. It reveals the content for what it is: text and images, rather than stimuli.

Strategic Reminder

Convenience is the enemy of focus. The easier it is to access the noise, the less value you place on the silence. Build walls. Make the cheap dopamine expensive.

Action: The Friction Rule

You don't actually make a conscious decision to check your feed.

Be honest. Most of the time, your thumb makes the decision for you. It happens in those tiny gaps between thoughts. You're waiting for the coffee to brew or a webpage to load, and suddenly, *tap*. You've already committed.

You didn't choose this. It was a reflex.

Silicon Valley spends billions of dollars to make that reflex possible. They call it 'frictionless design.' They want the slide from your boredom into their app to be as smooth as glass. Zero resistance. Zero thought.

And that is exactly where we have to break it.

We need to make your phone boring again.

This is the Rule of Friction. It's stupidly simple, but it works because it attacks your muscle memory instead of your willpower.

Take the apps that eat your time, the ones you open without even thinking, and burn them down.

Don't just remove them from your home screen. Put them in a folder. Then, put that folder inside another folder. Move that stack to the very last page of your interface.

Create a hassle.

Force yourself to swipe, tap, tap, and tap again just to see a photo of someone's lunch.

Watch what happens next.

When you reach for that icon, it isn't there. Your thumb hits nothing but empty glass. That split-second of confusion? That's the magic. That's the friction.

You're forced to wake up. You have to actively go looking for the app. And in the three seconds it takes to find it, your brain finally catches up. You get a window of time to ask yourself: *"Do I actually want to do this? Or was I just twitching?"*

Most of the time, it's just a twitch.

By adding just two extra clicks, you break the loop. You turn a mindless reflex back into a conscious choice.

And half the time, you'll realize it's simply not worth the effort. You'll just put the phone back down.

Case Snapshot: The Responder

Subject: David, 32. Product Manager.

Symptom: "I'm just staying on top of things."

David didn't think he had a problem. In fact, he was a high-performer. He was the guy who replied before you'd even finished typing your email. He was the one jumping into Slack threads to solve problems at 10:30 PM on a Tuesday.

He wore his responsiveness like a badge of honour. He called it "agility."

We installed a tracker on his laptop for one week. We didn't block anything; we didn't interrupt his flow. We just ran the numbers.

The data was undeniable: David checked Slack 87 times and his email 64 times in a single day. He was switching windows, toggling between his project tools, chat, and browser, every 3 minutes and 15 seconds.

When we showed him the log, he actually laughed. He thought the software was broken.

'There's no way,' he said. 'I spent all day yesterday on the strategic roadmap.'

He hadn't.

According to the timestamps, the longest continuous block of time David spent on his strategy document was just 11 minutes.

He wasn't working. He was being interrupted, mostly by himself."

David had fallen into the trap of confusing motion with progress. Each time a notification popped up, he got a tiny hit of dopamine, a small sense of being "needed." Answering a question felt like work. Forwarding a file felt like work.

But at the end of the week, his roadmap, the one thing that actually mattered, was still blank.

The Intervention: we enforced the 10-2-4 Rule. David was only allowed to check Slack at 10:00 AM, 2:00 PM, and 4:00 PM. He set up an auto-responder that read: *"I'm in Deep Work mode until 2:00 PM. If the building is on fire, call me."*

The Result: The first day was brutal. David suffered from "phantom vibrations" in his pocket. He felt a heavy wave of guilt, convinced he was letting his team down.

No one called. The building didn't burn down.

By Wednesday, the "emergencies" had simply evaporated. Because David wasn't there to solve every tiny hiccup instantly, his team actually started figuring things out on their own.

And the roadmap? David finished the entire thing in just two days.

He finally realized he hadn't been "agile" at all. He had just been loud.

CHAPTER 4: CODE YELLOW, THE MAINTENANCE

You know the feeling.

You sit down at your desk at 9:00 AM with the best intentions. You have that big project to finish, a report to write, a map to draft. You're ready to dive in.

But first, you tell yourself you just need to 'clear the deck.'

So, you open your email. You check Slack. You reply to a few messages, put out a tiny fire, forward a document, and schedule a meeting. You feel busy. You feel productive. You feel like a 'good employee.'

Then you look up. It's 11:30 AM.

Your energy is shot. The big project hasn't even been touched. And your inbox is already filling up again.

This is the trap of Code Yellow.

In our triage system, 'Code Yellow' isn't just mindless scrolling, but it's also not your most important work. It's maintenance, the logistical 'noise' and administrative overhead of modern life that constantly presses down on us.

To feel better, we tell ourselves we're 'working.' But the truth is, we're just reacting.

Here's the cold, hard truth about your inbox: Your email is actually a to-do list created by other people.

Every unread message is a demand. It's someone else, a client, a boss, or even a stranger, stepping into your day and claiming a piece of your time. They are prioritizing their needs over your output. When you start your day in your inbox, you've already surrendered your agenda. You're playing defence, letting the world dictate your minutes until you have no time left for yourself.

Most of us have spent our entire careers stuck in this loop. We mistake 'clearing the queue' for making real progress. We wear our constant responsiveness like a badge of honour.

'I'm on top of everything,' we tell ourselves.

But the truth is, you aren't on top of anything. You're just treading water, barely keeping your head above the surface.

Code Yellow is dangerous because it *feels* productive. It looks like work. But if you spend eight hours straight just answering emails, you haven't actually created anything. You haven't solved a single hard problem. You've just moved information from one place to another.

Simply put, you've acted as a high-paid human router.

We have to stop treating maintenance as the 'main event.' You have to shrink the box this work lives in. You have to fence it off, because if you don't, it will swallow every precious hour of your life.

The Mechanism

The Setup Tax

You operate under a false assumption. You believe that checking an email takes thirty seconds. You think: *"I'll just clear this one notification. It's quick. Then I'll go back to work."*

This is a calculation error.

You are accounting for the Execution Time (reading and typing), but you are ignoring the Setup Time.

In industrial manufacturing, every task has a fixed cost. If a factory wants to switch from making Car Part A to Car Part B, they have to stop the machines, swap the dies, and recalibrate the software. That is the "Setup." It takes time and burns fuel, but produces zero value.

Your brain works the same way.

For every single digital task, even a "quick" text, there is a cognitive setup process:

- o Shift visual focus.
- o Load the context (Who is this? What project is this regarding?).
- o Decide on the action.
- o Execute.

The Setup often costs more time than the task itself. The "Execution" might only take 10 seconds.

When you process emails one by one as they arrive, you are paying the Setup Tax every single time.

- Reply to 1 email = 1 Setup Tax + 1 Execution.
- Reply to 10 emails (individually) = 10 Setup Taxes + 10 Executions.

You are paying ten times the energy cost for the same output.

This is why you feel exhausted at 2:00 PM despite accomplishing very little. You are spending 90% of your energy on the *overhead* of switching, not the *work* itself.

Batching is one of the few reliable ways to reduce this tax.

When you save all your emails for a single "Code Yellow" block at 2:00 PM, you pay the Setup Tax exactly once. You enter "Email Mode." You calibrate your brain for administrative speed. Then, you execute fifty times in a row with zero friction.

- Reply to 50 emails (batched) = 1 Setup Tax + 50 Executions.

The factory manager never stops the assembly line to build one single car part. They build a thousand at a time. Stop stopping your line for every notification. Run the batch.

The Resistance

The Anxiety of the Queue

The primary friction against batching is not logistical. It is emotional.

When you stop checking your inbox every ten minutes, the number climbs. You watch the badge count go from 5 to 10 to 50.

For most professionals, this triggers a visceral alarm response. We have been conditioned to view an empty inbox as "safety" and a full inbox as "risk."

The Resistance whispers: *"If I let them pile up until 2:00 PM, I will be overwhelmed. It is better to clear them as they come to keep the number low."*

Analysis: This is a false metric.

You are confusing Inventory Management with Throughput.

Imagine a warehouse. If a truck arrives with 50 boxes, you have two choices:

- o Continuous Flow: You stop what you are doing, carry one box to the shelf, walk back, wait for the next box, carry it to the shelf, and repeat fifty times.
- o Batched Flow: You let the boxes pile up on the dock until all 50 are there. Then, you load a pallet and move them all at once.

Method 1 keeps the dock "clean," but it destroys your efficiency. You are walking back and forth fifty times. Method 2 looks messy, there is a pile of boxes on the dock! , but it is exponentially faster.

The "clean dock" is an illusion of control.

When you clear emails one by one, you are prioritizing the *appearance* of order over the *speed* of execution. You are soothing your anxiety about the pile, but you are slowing down the actual work.

The "Open Loop" Tension There is a psychological reason for this anxiety. It is called the Zeigarnik Effect. The human brain remembers uncompleted tasks better than completed ones. Unread emails sit in your working memory as "open loops," creating a subtle, nagging tension.

We check the inbox not to work, but to close the loop. We check to relieve the pressure of the unknown.

"Who is emailing me? Is it a problem? Is it my boss?"

However, this relief is temporary. As soon as you clear one loop, another arrives.

The Caged Monster You must reframe the backlog.

A pile of 50 unread emails looks like a monster. But it is a Caged Monster.

When you attack the emails one by one throughout the day, the monster is roaming free. It interrupts you constantly. It controls your schedule. It taps you on the shoulder whenever it wants. When you force the emails to wait for your 2:00 PM block, you have put the monster in a cage.

It might growl. The number might get high. But it cannot hurt you.

You are safer with 50 unread emails in a cage than with 1 unread email that is allowed to walk into your meeting.

The goal is not to keep the number at zero. The goal is to keep the monsters in the containment unit until *you* are ready to deal with them.

You must learn to tolerate the discomfort of the queue. The unread count is not a measure of your failure. It is a measure of your focus elsewhere.

Let the number climb. It is safe.

The Toolkit

The Auto-Responder Defence

The primary failure point of batching is Expectation Mismanagement.

If you suddenly stop replying to emails instantly, your colleagues will assume something is wrong. They will think you are sick, angry, or slacking. They will start texting you: *"Did you get my email?"*

You cannot just vanish. You must broadcast the new protocol.

Present it as an operational adjustment. State the protocol as an operational update.

The "Deep Work" Auto-Responder

Most professionals only use "Out of Office" replies when they are on vacation. This is a waste of a powerful tool. You should use an auto-responder daily to create a defensive buffer.

The Script (Internal/External):

"Thanks for the email. I am currently checking messages twice a day (at 10:00 AM and 3:00 PM) to prioritize deep project work.

If this is a true emergency that cannot wait until the next window, please call my cell at [Number].

Otherwise, I will respond during the next batch.

Why this works:

- o It defines the terms: The sender knows exactly *when* to expect a reply, which eliminates the anxiety of silence. They stop chasing you.

- It creates a filter: By offering your cell number for "emergencies," you force them to make a high-friction choice: *"Is this actually worth a phone call?"*
    - In practice, most issues can wait.

The Slack Status Protocol

Slack is a presence-based tool. It demands to know if you are "Active." If you simply close the app, your dot turns grey. To a manager, grey looks like "Offline." It looks like you went home.

Use the Status feature to signal "Focused," not "Absent."

The Status Setting: *Focus Mode | Checking @ 11am & 4pm*

This subtle distinction is critical. "Offline" implies you are not working. "Focus Mode" signals that you are prioritizing execution. It signals intensity.

The "Send Later" Protocol

When you process your email batch (e.g., at 4:30 PM), do not send all the replies instantly.

If you send 20 emails at 4:30 PM, you will trigger 20 immediate replies at 4:35 PM. You will create a new wave of noise just as you are trying to finish your day. You are inviting a ping-pong match.

Use the "Schedule Send" feature.

- Process the entire batch.
- Draft every reply.
- Schedule them to arrive tomorrow morning at 9:15 AM.

This allows you to clear your queue mentally without reopening the loop socially. You finish the day at Zero, but you protect your evening from the rebound.

The "Touch It Once" Rule

During a Code Yellow batch, you are not allowed to "check" emails. You are only allowed to "process" them.

If you open an email, you must perform one of three actions immediately:

- o Delete/Archive: It is noise.
- o Reply: It takes less than 2 minutes. Do it now.
- o Task: It requires real work. Move it to your To-Do list (or project management tool) and archive the email.

The Rule: You never close an email and leave it in the inbox "for later." That is essentially shuffling papers on a desk. It is motion, not progress. If you touch it, you must move it.

Strategic Reminder

Responsiveness is a service you provide. Like any service, it must have operating hours. If a store is open 24/7, it is a convenience store. If it has limited hours, it is a boutique. Be the boutique. Set the hours.

Action 1: The 10-2-4 Rule

You're probably keeping that tab open.

Right now, it's just sitting there in the corner of your screen. Maybe there's a tiny red number next to it, slowly climbing. You tell yourself you're multitasking. You think being available the second a message hits makes you efficient.

It doesn't.

You're playing a dangerous game.

Every time you switch contexts just to answer a 'quick question,' your focus shatters. You are trading away a piece of your brain's potential for a cheap hit of 'feeling busy.'

Stop.

"Close the tab. Shut down the app.

We're moving to a batching schedule. It's called the 10-2-4 Rule.

It works exactly like it sounds. You process all your communications, emails, Slack, messages, at three specific times:

- **10:00 AM**
- **2:00 PM**
- **4:00 PM**

That's your window. Outside of those times, the shop is closed.

This works because:

- 10:00 AM gives you your morning back. You don't start the day in 'reactive mode.' You spend the first two hours doing your own deep, high-impact work before ever opening the gates to the outside noise.

- o 2:00 PM catches the post-lunch drift. It's the perfect time to reset, check in on urgent requests, and keep projects moving after your midday break.
- o 4:00 PM is the 'cleanup crew.' You clear the decks and answer the final demands of the day, allowing you to log out with a clear conscience and zero guilt.

Research on context switching consistently shows that it drains far more energy than we realize.

I know what you're thinking, how will people react if you don't answer them immediately?

I can't do that. People expect a reply right away."

Are you sure? Or have you just trained them to expect it?

When you reply to an email within thirty seconds, you're teaching that person that you're just sitting there, waiting for them. You're signalling that their random thought is more important than your actual work. You set that standard. You can reset it.

Most things aren't emergencies. If the server crashes, they'll call you. If the building is on fire, the alarm will go off. Everything else? It can wait until 2:00 PM.

Letting messages pile up feels risky, like you're losing control. But you aren't. You're just letting the laundry stack up so you can wash it all at once, instead of running the machine for a single sock.

Close the tab.

Action 2: The Template Library

You're repeating yourself.

If you tracked every single keystroke you made this week, you'd find a pattern. You are typing the same five sentences over and over again.

Thanks for reaching out.' 'I'll take a look and get back to you.' 'Can we push this to Tuesday?' 'Please see the attached document.'

You type them out yourself. You try to be polite. You tweak the wording just a bit so you don't sound like a machine.

Stop.

Be the machine.

The issue isn't your typing speed, it's the emotional tax.

Every time you draft a "polite decline" or a "schedule update," you're burning through a small amount of your creative fuel. You worry about the tone. You second-guess yourself, wondering if you sound too abrupt or cold.

You are wasting high-grade intelligence on low-value logistics.

Think about the response once, perfect it, and then never think about it again.

This is the Template Protocol.

Go through your Sent folder. Find the three emails you send most often. Maybe it's the "No, I can't take this on right now" email, or the "Here are the instructions" guide.

Write the perfect version of it. Make it warm, make it crystal clear, and make it bulletproof.

Then, lock it in. Store it in your email's "Signature" settings, use a Text Expander tool, or even just keep a simple Word doc on your desktop.

Next time the request comes in?

Click.

It's gone.

You didn't have to overthink it. You didn't have to summon the willpower to be 'nice' for the tenth time today. You just pushed a button.

This isn't laziness. It's professionalism.

Architects don't redraw the brick every time they design a wall; they use a standard. Your words are tools. Sharpen them once, and then use them to build something that actually matters.

Stop spending your creativity on your inbox. Save it for the blank page.

CHAPTER 5: CODE RED, PROTECTING THE VITALS

You could be busy for ten hours a day.

You can reply to every email within five minutes. You can attend every single meeting. You can be the most responsive, reliable, 'always-on' person in your department. You can scrub your to-do list until it sparkles.

And at the end of the year, you'll have achieved nothing.

You've maintained the status quo. You kept the lights on. You moved information from Pile A to Pile B.

That isn't work. That's administration.

There is a massive difference between motion and progress.

In the Triage Protocol, Code Red cases are the ones that truly matter. It's the gunshot wound. The cardiac arrest. The emergency surgery that demands 100% of the team's focus, skill, and intensity.

When a surgeon is deep inside a chest cavity, no one taps them on the shoulder to ask if they've seen the memo about the office holiday party. No one hands them a phone to check a notification. The world stops. The doors are locked. The focus is total.

Why? Because if they lose focus, the cost is real."

In your life, Code Red is the work that actually moves the needle.

This is the strategic document that pivots the entire company. It's the breakthrough code that clears the roadblock. It's the chapter of your book. It's that difficult, honest conversation with your child.

This is the hard, scary, high-impact stuff.

And let's be honest: most of us avoid Code Red. We run from it.

We hide in our inboxes because the inbox is easy, it tells us exactly what to do. But Code Red is demanding. It forces you to stare at a blank page or a complex problem and pull the answer out of your own head.

It's painful. It burns through your mental fuel. It feels risky.

So we procrastinate. We do "maintenance." We polish the slides. We reorganize our folders. We clear out the easy emails.

But here is the reality: No one pays you for your inbox.

They pay you for your judgment. They pay you for your creativity. They pay you to solve the problems that a computer script cannot solve.

If you don't carve out time for the vitals, If you don't treat your deep work with that level of protection, you risk becoming reactive instead of strategic. You're just a highly skilled caretaker. You're watching the needle, but you aren't moving it.

The Mechanism

The RAM Wipe

You think of your focus like a pause button. You believe that if you stop writing a strategy document to answer a quick text, you can just press "play" and pick up right where you left off.

That assumption doesn't match how cognition works.

Your brain does not have a hard drive for active thought. It has RAM (Random Access Memory).

When you are doing "Code Red" work, writing code, designing a complex system, or solving a math problem, you are not just "thinking." You are loading a massive, fragile structure of variables into your short-term memory. You are holding the beginning of the sentence, the logic of the paragraph, the data from the spreadsheet, and the goal of the project all in suspension at the same time.

This is called State.

Building "State" takes time. It takes time to build that state to load all those variables into your RAM until you can manipulate them fluently.

But RAM is volatile. It requires constant power to maintain the data.

When you check a text message, you are not just "pausing." You are cutting the power to that specific circuit.

Because your working memory is extremely limited, your brain has to dump the complex data of your project to load the new data of the text message.

It is a RAM Wipe.

The structure destabilizes. The house of cards falls down.

When you return to the work ten seconds later, you feel that familiar, groggy confusion. *"Where was I? What was I trying to say?"*

You aren't just "distracted." You are rebuilding. You have to spend another 15 minutes reloading the variables one by one just to get back to the state you were in before the ping.

If you allow a "quick check" every ten minutes, you are effectively wiping your RAM every time you almost reach full capacity. You are running a high-performance machine that is constantly rebooting.

This is why you can spend eight hours "working" but only produce one hour of value. You weren't working. You were reloading.

The Resistance

The Fear of the Void

The primary friction against Deep Work is rarely laziness. It is Fear of the Silence.

When you strip away the emails, the Slack notifications, and the administrative busywork, you are left with just two things:

- o Your brain.
- o The problem.

There is no noise to hide behind. There is no "admin" to make you feel productive.

This creates a specific type of anxiety called The Vacuum.

In the Vacuum, you are forced to confront the limits of your own ability. You have to generate an output from scratch. That is scary. It is much easier to reply to a question (reactive) than to solve a blank page (generative).

So, the Resistance whispers: *"I need to check my email just to make sure I have all the context before I start."* Or: *"I'll just clear these three small tasks to get some momentum."*

Analysis: Often, it's avoidance disguised as preparation.

You are filling the Vacuum with noise because the noise feels safe. The noise validates you ("I am busy, therefore I am good"). Deep work exposes uncertainty ("Here is the problem, can you solve it?").

The Agitation Phase You must learn to tolerate the initial discomfort of the Void.

The first 10 minutes of a Code Red block will always feel like agitation. You will feel restless. You will want to bolt. You will reach for the phone.

This is not a sign that you are "distracted." It is a sign that your brain is shifting gears.

Think of it like a cold engine. It rattles before it hums. The agitation is just the friction of the loading phase.

If you give in to the urge to "check" something, you kill the engine. You relieve the tension, but you destroy the warm-up.

The practice is simple: remain in place.

When the agitation hits, sit with it. Stare at the blank screen. Boredom is the threshold of depth.

If you stay in the chair for fifteen minutes without stimulation, the noise will settle. The RAM will load. The agitation will be replaced by traction.

But you have to pay the toll of boredom to enter the city of focus.

Most people aren't willing to pay. They turn back to the inbox because it's cheaper.

The Toolkit

The Bunker Protocol

We cannot rely on "willpower" to maintain a Code Red state. Willpower is a battery; it drains with every decision you make to ignore a distraction. We need to remove the decision entirely.

The Hardware Air Gap

Do not just silence the phone. Remove connectivity temporarily. When you enter a Code Red block, toggle Airplane Mode on your phone.

Why Airplane Mode? Because "Do Not Disturb" is software. You know, deep down, that you can bypass it with a swipe. Your brain knows the connection is still live. Airplane Mode is hardware logic. It cuts the radio. It reduces the sense of potential interruption, *"The world literally cannot reach me right now."*

This silences the "potentiality" loop. You stop wondering *if* someone texted you, because you know they *can't*.

Zero-Interface Protocol

Your Operating System is not a neutral background. It is a dashboard of competitors. The clock, the battery percentage, the wifi signal, the bouncing dock icons, these are all data points. Every time your eye catches the time (10:42 AM), your brain performs a subconscious calculation: *"How much time is left? Am I behind? When is lunch?"*

That calculation costs energy.

The Strategy: Eliminate the "Chrome." (In design, "chrome" is the interface that surrounds the content).

Force your application into Native Full Screen. Push the work until it touches all four corners of the physical monitor. Minimize visible interface elements where possible. If you can see the battery, you are wrong. If you can see another tab, you are wrong.

The only pixels on the screen should be the problem you are solving.

The "Burner" Browser

If your work requires the internet, you are walking through a minefield. Your primary browser carries behavioural associations. It remembers your passwords. It knows your search history. It is logged into your email.

Opening a new tab in your main browser is like trying to work in a casino. The slot machines are right there.

The Strategy: Use a Sanitized Environment.

Install a secondary browser that you *never* use for personal life.

- No bookmarks.
- No saved passwords.
- No history.
- No cookies.

This is your Work Browser. When you open it, the algorithm doesn't know who you are. YouTube doesn't recommend videos. Twitter doesn't auto-login.

It is a cold, sterile tool. Use it to find the specific fact you need, paste it into your work, and close it. Do not let your "Life" browser and your "Work" browser touch. Keep contexts separate.

The Timer Authority

You are your own worst manager. You will negotiate with yourself to quit early. *"I've done enough. I'm stuck. I'll just check email for a second."*

Do not negotiate. Outsource the authority.

Set a physical timer for 90 minutes.

The Rule: You are not allowed to solve the problem in that time. You are only required to *sit with it.* You can stare at the wall. You can nap. You can write. But you cannot check email. You cannot switch tasks. You cannot leave the chair.

When the timer is running, the decision is made. You are in a protected block. When the timer beeps, you are free.

Strategic Reminder

Deep work tolerates very little fragmentation. You are either in the tunnel, or you are out of it. There is no "halfway." You cannot be 90% in a deep dive and 10% checking texts. That 10% destroys the structure. Protect the RAM.

Action 1: The Golden Hours

Stop pretending you are a machine.

You don't have eight hours of focus in you. Nobody does.

The industrial revolution convinced us that 9:00 AM is the same as 4:00 PM. It lied.

If you are moving bricks, sure. One hour of lifting is the same as the next. But you aren't moving bricks. You are moving ideas. And for that kind of work, your energy isn't a flat line. It's a wave.

You have a specific window, maybe two or three hours a day, where you are sharp.

You know when it is.

For most people, it's the morning. It's that crisp window between the first coffee and the first lunch meeting. For night owls, it might be 10:00 PM.

These are your Golden Hours.

During this time, your brain is expensive. It is high-performance. You can solve a problem in twenty minutes that would take you two hours to slog through in the afternoon.

And what do most of us do with this premium, high-value time?

We give it away.

We spend our Golden Hours sitting in status meetings. We spend them clearing out the inbox. We spend them on Slack.

We take our best energy, the only energy capable of doing Code Red work, and we burn it on Code Yellow maintenance.

This is a tragedy.

It's like using a flamethrower to light a birthday candle. It works, but what a waste of fuel.

The Protocol:

Find your peak. Be honest about it.

If you are sharpest at 9:00 AM, that time is now sacred. Block it on your calendar. Label it "Deep Work" or "Strategy."

Do not accept meetings during this block. Do not check email during this block.

Use this time *only* for the hardest thing you have to do today. The thing that requires 100% of you.

Save the email for 3:00 PM. Save the meetings for the afternoon slump. When your brain is tired and foggy, *that* is the time to do the admin. You can reply to an email when you're half-asleep. You can sit in a Zoom call when you're drained.

But you cannot create when you are empty.

Guard the gold. Spend the loose change on the rest.

Action 2: The Single-Task Protocol

You've seen the setups.

Maybe you have one.

Three monitors. A vertical screen for code or chat. A horizontal one for email. A main display for "work." It looks like the cockpit of a fighter jet. It looks serious. It makes you feel like a high-powered trader or a hacker in a movie.

It's a trap.

That "Command Center" isn't optimizing your output. It's optimizing your distraction.

We have convinced ourselves that seeing everything at once means we are controlling everything at once. But you aren't.

You can't read two things at the same time. You can't write a sentence while reading a Slack message.

When you have three screens open, you aren't multitasking. You are just twitching.

Your eyes are darting from the document to the notification badge on the left, then to the email ticker on the right. Every single glance is a micro-interruption. It breaks the thread. You drop the heavy thought you were holding to pick up a light one, and then you have to heave the heavy one back up again.

This is why you feel exhausted at 2:00 PM. You didn't run a marathon. You just spent six hours switching gears.

The Rule: One Monitor. One Tab. One Goal.

When you enter Code Red, you need tunnel vision.

If you are writing, the only thing on your screen should be the words.

If you are analyzing data, the only thing should be the spreadsheet.

Turn off the second monitor. Physically unplug it if you have to. Close the browser tabs that "might be useful later." (They won't be. You can open them again in two hours).

Make your digital world the size of a postage stamp.

When there is nowhere else to look, you are forced to look at the work. You are forced to push through the hard part because there is no easy distraction sitting in your peripheral vision offering you an escape.

It feels claustrophobic at first. You'll reach for the "check" reflex, and you'll hit a wall.

Good.

Stay in the tunnel. That is where the work gets done.

PHASE 3: PREVENTING RE-INFECTION

Case Snapshot: The Hoarder

Subject: Elena, 45. VP of Operations. The Symptom: "It's organized chaos. I know where everything is."

Elena's computer screen looked like a war zone.

There was no wallpaper visible. Just icons. Hundreds of them. Layers of screenshots, PDF contracts, half-finished spreadsheets, and "read later" articles from three years ago.

She called it her "dashboard."

"If I file it away," she said, *"I'll forget to do it. I need to see it."*

She believed that keeping the files on the desktop was a memory aid. She thought she was keeping her tasks front-and-center.

She wasn't. She was building a wall.

The Diagnosis: Elena was suffering from Visual Noise.

Every single icon on that screen was a tiny, subconscious scream for attention. Every time she minimized a window to check her email, her brain had to process 400 unfinished tasks in a fraction of a second.

She wasn't "seeing" the files. She was flinching at them.

It was creating a low-grade background anxiety. She felt heavy before she even typed a word. She felt behind schedule the moment she logged in.

She didn't have a storage problem. She had a decision problem.

The Intervention: We didn't organize the files. We didn't create a complex folder structure with colour codes.

We used the Nuclear Option.

1. We created a single folder on the desktop.
2. We named it: "OLD_DESKTOP_[Date]".
3. We selected every single icon, all 432 of them.
4. We dragged them into the folder.

The Result: The screen was empty. Just a clean, blue background.

Elena panicked.

"I can't see anything," she said. *"I don't know what to do."*

"Exactly," I said. *"Now you have to decide what to do."*

For the first time in a decade, Elena opened her laptop and saw... nothing. No guilt. No past. No "should have done this."

She had to actively choose which project to open. She had to pull the work *out* of the archive, instead of having the archive scream at her.

She realized that "out of sight" didn't mean "out of mind."

It meant "out of the way."

CHAPTER 6: DIGITAL HYGIENE ROUTINES

You clean your kitchen on Sunday. By Wednesday, there are crumbs on the counter. By Friday, there are dishes in the sink.

You don't panic. You don't scream, "My kitchen is broken!" You don't blame the architecture of the house.

You just wash the dishes.

It's just life. Things get messy. Entropy is the only law that never takes a day off.

Yet, with our digital lives, we expect a miracle.

We do a big purge in January. We organize the files. We clear the desktop. We unsubscribe from the newsletters. We feel virtuous. We think, *"Finally. I am organized."*

Then, three weeks later, the desktop is covered in screenshots. The inbox has 400 unread messages. The "Read Later" folder is a graveyard of things you will never read.

And we think, *"I failed. The system didn't work."*

The system didn't fail. You just stopped doing the maintenance.

Digital clutter is not a sign of weakness. It is a byproduct of activity. If you are doing work, you are making a mess. You are downloading files. You are signing up for things. You are creating temporary loops.

That is fine.

The problem isn't the mess. The problem is that you treat the mess as a surprise.

You cannot "fix" your digital life once and for all. You can only manage it.

In a hospital, sterilization isn't a one-time event. They don't scrub the operating room in 1995 and say, *"Well, that should hold us for a while."*

They scrub it after every single surgery. They have a protocol. They have a rhythm.

If you want the Sterile Field to hold, you have to scrub up. You need a routine that accounts for the chaos, expects it, and resets it before it calcifies into a permanent wall of noise.

You need a hygiene cycle.

The Mechanism

Digital Entropy (The Barnacle Effect)

You treat organization as a project. You think, *"I will clean up my computer this weekend,"* and you assume that once it is clean, it will stay clean.

That assumption misunderstands how systems behave over time.

You are fighting Entropy. The Second Law of Thermodynamics applies to your hard drive just as much as it applies to the universe: Chaos is the default state. Order requires energy.

Every time you download a file, take a screenshot, or install an app, you are introducing a new variable into the system. You are increasing the complexity.

Most people ignore this complexity because digital clutter is weightless. If you hoarded newspapers in your living room, you would trip over them. You would smell them. The environment would force you to clean. But a "Downloads" folder with 4,000 files takes up zero physical space. It is invisible.

So you let it slide.

This creates The Barnacle Effect.

A ship does not sink because of barnacles. It just gets slow. As the hull accumulates tiny, hard shells, the drag coefficient increases. The engine has to work harder to push the ship through the water at the same speed. Eventually, The engine works harder for the same speed.

Your digital environment works the same way.

- Search Friction: When you have 5,000 files on your desktop,

"Spotlight Search" takes longer. You take longer to find the contract.

- o Decision Drag: When your "To-Do" app is filled with tasks from 2021, you stop trusting the list. You have to mentally filter the old junk to find the new reality.
- o Visual Noise: When your browser has 50 bookmarks you never read, you stop using bookmarks.

You aren't crashing. You are just dragging.

You are burning more cognitive fuel to achieve the same result. You feel "slow" not because you are getting older, but because your operating system is covered in three years of unaddressed friction.

You cannot "fix" entropy once a year. If you wait until the system is broken to fix it, the system will feel heavier than it should. You must flush the system *before* the drag becomes noticeable.

Hygiene is not about being "neat." It is about aerodynamics.

The Resistance

The Janitor Fallacy

The primary friction against digital hygiene is Productivity Guilt.

When you spend thirty minutes renaming files, archiving old projects, or clearing your downloads folder, you feel a pang of anxiety. Your brain whispers: *"You are wasting time. You should be sending emails. You should be building the deck. This is janitor work."*

You view maintenance as Negative Work. You see it as time subtracted from your "real" output.

So you defer it. *"I'll organize the server later." "I'll clean up the desktop when this project is done."*

Analysis: This is a short-term calculation.

Professionals do not view maintenance as a subtraction. They view it as a multiplier.

Look at a professional chef. Before a single customer walks in, the chef spends hours on *Mise-en-place*. They chop the onions. They organize the spices. They sharpen the knives. They do not say, *"I don't have time to sharpen my knife; I have to cook."* They know that if the knife is dull, the cooking takes twice as long.

When you skip the hygiene to "get to work," you are cooking with a dull knife.

The Search Tax You are ignoring the invisible cost of the mess: Search Latency.

Every time you save a file to the desktop named "Untitled_Final_v2," you are creating a future debt. Three weeks from now, when you need that file in a crisis, you will spend 15 minutes clicking through folders, searching your email, and panicking.

- Hygiene Cost: 10 seconds to name it correctly today.
- Chaos Cost: 10 minutes to find it next month.

You are trading a moment of friction for a month of drag. You are saving seconds now to waste hours later.

The Resistance tells you that you are "too busy" to organize. The reality is that disorganization often creates the busyness we later complain about.

You are not a janitor cleaning up a mess. You are a pit crew mechanic tuning the engine so the car doesn't explode on the next lap.

There's no need to frame maintenance as wasted time.

The Toolkit

The Closing Shift Protocol

We treat our digital workspace like a teenager's bedroom: we leave the mess until it becomes unbearable, and then we spend a frantic Saturday cleaning it up. This approach is unsustainable.

We need to operate like a professional kitchen. A chef never leaves a dirty station at the end of the night. Even if they are exhausted, they wipe the counters, sharpen the knives, and prep the *mise-en-place* for the morning crew.

You are the morning crew. Do not sabotage your future self.

The 10-Minute Closing Shift

At the end of every workday, before you close your laptop, execute this sequence. It takes exactly ten minutes.

- Close All Tabs: Close them all at once. If a tab is important, bookmark it. If it is a task, add it to your To-Do list. Do not leave tabs open as "reminders." That is just cognitive debt.
- Clear the Desktop: Move every loose file into the "Inbox" folder or delete it.
- Empty the Trash: Psychologically, this signals "Day Complete."
- Shut Down (Don't Sleep): Rebooting clears the RAM and resets the system caches. It forces a fresh start.

When you open your laptop tomorrow morning, you will see a clean, silent slate. You will start with *momentum*, not maintenance.

Downloads Reset

Your "Downloads" folder is a graveyard of PDF menus, installer files, and accidental duplicates. It is where focus goes to die.

The Rule: The Downloads folder is a Transfer Station, not a Storage Unit.

Treat it like a physical mailbox. You take the mail *out* and walk it into the house. You don't live in the mailbox.

The Protocol: Every Friday at 4:00 PM (during your Code Yellow block), open Downloads.

- o Sort by "Date Added".
- o Keep: Anything from the last 24 hours that you are actively processing.
- o File: Anything you actually need for a project (move it to the project folder immediately).
- o Delete: Everything else.

A useful threshold: If a file has been in Downloads for more than 7 days, it is trash. Delete it. If it was important, you would have filed it.

The ISO Naming Convention

Search is broken because your naming is lazy. If you name a file final_draft_v2.docx, you will never find it in six months. You will have fifty files with that name.

Adopt the ISO 8601 standard. Format: YYYY-MM-DD_Description_Context

- o *Bad:* Meeting Notes.txt
- o *Good:* 2023-10-27_MeetingNotes_Q4Strategy.txt

Why? Because computers sort numbers logically. This format forces your files to sort chronologically by default, regardless of when you last opened them. It makes "Search" instant. You don't have to remember *what* you wrote; you only have to remember *when* it happened.

The "Update" Window

Software updates are friction. They pop up when you are in flow, and you click "Remind Me Tomorrow." You have been clicking "Remind Me Tomorrow" for three months.

This creates technical debt. It slows down the OS and leaves security holes.

The Protocol: Sunday Morning (or Friday Afternoon).

- Schedule a weekly update window and run all system updates at once

Do not do this during the week. Do it when the machine is idle. Keep the tools sharp.

Strategic Reminder

A clean workspace is not about aesthetics. It is about reduced drag. Every second you spend searching for a file is a second you are not building the future. Reset to zero every single day.

Action: The Friday Flush

It's 4:55 PM on a Friday.

You are done. Your brain is toast. You just want to slam the laptop shut, grab a drink, and forget the last five days happened.

So you do.

You leave the twenty tabs open. You leave the random PDFs scattered across the desktop. You leave the half-written email in the drafts folder.

You tell yourself, *"I'll deal with it on Monday."*

You just ruined your weekend.

You might not feel it immediately. But somewhere in the back of your mind, those open loops are still spinning. That clutter is a subconscious weight. It's the reason you get that knot in your stomach on Sunday night. You know, deep down, that you are walking back into a disaster zone.

Monday morning is hard enough. Don't make it start with an apology to yourself.

You need a shut-down ritual.

We call this The Friday Flush.

Set a timer. Fifteen minutes. That's it. You aren't reorganizing the entire hard drive. You are just taking out the trash.

1. The Downloads Folder. This is your digital junk drawer. It is full of installers, temporary screenshots, and restaurant menus. Open it. *Select All.* Delete. If there is a tax document in there, move it. For everything else? If you haven't used it by Friday, you don't need it.

2. The Browser Tabs. Be ruthless here. If a tab is an article you "meant to read," you aren't going to read it. Close it. If it is a task you didn't finish, write it down on a physical sticky note and stick it to your keyboard. Then close the tab. Your browser should be a blank slate.

3. The Desktop. Sweep it. Move the files to the "Archive" folder or the trash. When you open your computer on Monday, you should see a clean, empty background.

There is a profound dignity in closing the shop properly.

When you scrub the deck, you are drawing a hard line between "Work" and "Rest." You are telling your brain, *"We are finished."*

You walk away light.

And when you sit down on Monday with your coffee, and you open a pristine, silent screen?

You will thank Friday You for having your back.

Case Snapshot: The Curator

Subject: Sarah, 29. Senior Art Director. The Symptom: "I just need to find some inspiration first."

Sarah wasn't lazy. She was tasteful.

She had impeccable folders on Pinterest. She followed the top 50 design agencies on Instagram. She had a "Swipe File" that would make a museum curator jealous.

Every morning, she sat down to design a brand identity, and the first thing she did was open a tab.

"Just looking for references," she said.

Two hours later, she was deep in a hole of typography trends from 1970s Japan. She felt productive because she was looking at beautiful things. She felt like she was working because she was analyzing colour palettes.

But her own canvas was blank.

The Diagnosis: Sarah was suffering from Input Toxicity.

She had consumed so much high-quality work from other people that she was terrified to make a mark. Every time she had a nascent idea, she immediately compared it to the polished, finished, algorithm-selected masterpieces on her feed.

And her idea lost. Every time.

She wasn't researching. She was intimidating herself.

She had traded *creation* for *curation*. It feels safer to organize other people's genius than to risk displaying your own mediocrity.

The Intervention: We applied a strict "Output First" Protocol.

- o No Reference Material for the first 90 minutes of the day.
- o Wifi Off.
- o She had to sketch 10 bad ideas on paper before she was allowed to open a browser.

The Result: The first three days were excruciating. Sarah sat in silence. She felt empty. She realized she had forgotten how to generate an idea without a prompt.

"I have nothing," she told me.

"Good," I said. *"Boredom is where the ideas live."*

On Day 4, she drew a terrible logo. It was ugly. It was unbalanced.

But it was hers.

By the second week, the "reference addiction" broke. She stopped trying to mimic the feed and started trusting her hand.

She realized that inspiration isn't something you find on a screen. It's something you build when there is nowhere else to look.

CHAPTER 7: THE ALGORITHM DEFENCE

It feels like they are listening to you.

You mention a brand of shoes in a conversation, and ten minutes later, there is an ad for them. You feel a vague sense of anxiety about the news, and suddenly your feed is full of doom-scrolling headlines.

It feels creepy. It feels predatory.

But it isn't magic. It's just observation.

The algorithm isn't a mind reader. It is simply a very, very attentive student.

It watches your thumb. It measures exactly how many milliseconds you hesitated on that photo. It noticed that you clicked on the outrage bait at 11:00 PM last Tuesday. It saw that you watched the fight video all the way to the end, but scrolled past the cooking tutorial in two seconds.

And it drew a conclusion.

"This person wants more fights."

"This person wants to be angry."

We like to think of the algorithm as this dark, controlling force that force-feeds us garbage.

But that's not entirely true.

The algorithm is a mirror.

If your feed is full of shallow, noisy, infuriating content, it is because, at some point, you asked for it. You clicked. You engaged. You taught the machine that this is who you are.

Your feed is a confession.

That is the bad news.

Here is the good news: Anything that can be learned can be unlearned.

You are not a passive victim here. You are the trainer.

Every time you interact with your screen, you are conducting a training session. You are rewarding or punishing the software. When you hate-watch a video that makes your blood boil, you are giving the algorithm a treat. You are saying, *"Good boy. Do it again."*

So stop feeding the beast.

If you want a different digital life, you have to start teaching the machine new rules. You have to be intentional. You have to discipline your feed the same way you would discipline a pet that jumps on the furniture.

You can't just ignore the bad content. You have to actively reject it. And you have to aggressively reward the signal you actually want to see.

Don't let the algorithm tell you who you are.

Tell it who you want to be.

The Mechanism

The Radicalization Loop

You believe that your social media feed is a reflection of the world. You scroll through Twitter or Instagram and think: *"Everyone is so angry right now."* or *"The world is falling apart."*

That perception is incomplete.

The feed is not a window. It is a mirror. But it is a distorted mirror designed to reflect your own limbic system back at you.

The algorithm has one single directive: Maximize Time on Device. Its objective is retention, not balance or nuance.

Through billions of iterations of A/B testing, the machine learned a fundamental truth about human biology: a predictable pattern in human behaviour.

If you see a photo of a puppy, you smile, double-tap, and keep scrolling. (Interaction time: 1.5 seconds). If you see a post that attacks your political identity, insults your intelligence, or threatens your worldview, you stop. You read the comments. You feel your heart rate spike. You type a reply. (Interaction time: 45 seconds).

The algorithm notices this discrepancy. It marks the "puppy" as low-value content. It marks the "outrage" as high-value content.

So, it feeds you more outrage.

It is Reinforcement Learning. Every time you pause on a rage-bait post, you are training the machine. You are telling it: *"You are reinforcing the pattern."*

This creates a Feedback Loop of Extremes.

To keep your attention, the machine must escalate the stimulus. Yesterday's mild annoyance doesn't trigger you anymore. So today, it must show you something more radical, more polarizing, more terrifying.

You aren't seeing "the news." You are seeing a curated playlist of your own worst triggers.

You are not being informed. You are being exposed to increasingly extreme material. It is an engine that converts heightened emotional engagement into revenue.

The moment you understand that the "chaos" you see is artificially amplified to keep you staring at the screen, you realize the only winning move is to break the loop. You cannot reform the system from within. You must limit exposure.

The Resistance

The Fear of Irrelevance

The primary friction against disconnecting from the feed is the Fear of Missing Out (FOMO), but not in the way you think. It isn't just about missing a party. It is about missing the *culture.*

We consume the feed, the news snippets, the memes, the trending outrages, because we view them as the currency of connection. We worry that if we step out of the stream, we will have nothing to say to our colleagues. We fear becoming "the person who doesn't know."

This is a valid status calculation. In many circles, being "plugged in" is a proxy for being sharp.

The Resistance argues: *"But I need to be informed to be a responsible citizen/professional. Ignorance is dangerous."*

Analysis: You are confusing being Current with being Informed.

- Being Current requires constant, low-latency monitoring of a feed. It is a full-time job with zero output. It is knowing *what* just happened five minutes ago.
- Being Informed requires deep consumption of synthesized analysis, usually days or weeks after the event, when the facts are verified. It is knowing *why* it matters.

Most "breaking news" is Noise. It is ephemeral. It is highly emotional and often factually incomplete. It is relevant at 9:00 AM and obsolete by 4:00 PM. Investing your cognitive resources in retaining it is a poor allocation of memory.

When you step out of the stream, you do not become ignorant. You become selective.

You will miss the meme of the day. You will miss the initial wave of outrage. You might not know the trending hashtag.

But in exchange, you regain the capacity for Synthesis. You stop trading in the low-value currency of "what just happened" and start trading in the high-value currency of "what it means."

The initial feeling of isolation is not a defect. It is the system recalibrating. You are switching from a diet of fast food (high volume, low nutrient) to a diet of slow food (low volume, high nutrient).

The people who are "always online" are usually the ones with the shallowest understanding of the actual events. They have the headlines, but they lack the context.

Disconnection may feel uncomfortable at first. The signal will find you. The noise will filter itself out. You are not hiding from the world; you are waiting for the world to make sense before you let it in.

The Toolkit

The Feedless Interface

The system is optimized for engagement. It will usually outlast willpower, faster than you, and it never sleeps. If you fight it with willpower, you will lose. You must fight it with Architecture.

We need to dismantle the infinite scroll and replace it with finite endpoints.

Deploy the Feed Eradicator

On your desktop browser, the "News Feed" is a productivity killer. It is designed to hijack your attention the moment you log in to check a message or look up a contact.

The Strategy: Remove the feed interface.

Install a browser extension like "News Feed Eradicator." These tools replace the central algorithmic feed (on Facebook, LinkedIn, Twitter, YouTube) with a blank space or a simple inspiring quote.

The functionality of the site remains. You can still message people. You can still post. You can still visit specific profiles. But the *trap* is gone. You are no longer reacting to a stream of random stimuli. You are using the tool with Intent. You go in, do your job, and get out.

The "Mute" Protocol (Silent Curating)

"Unfollowing" people creates social friction. It signals a severed relationship. "Muting" people creates algorithmic silence without the drama.

The Strategy: Deliberate muting.

If a connection posts content that triggers anxiety, outrage, or envy, even if you like them personally, Mute them immediately. Do not hesitate.

Your feed is a diet. If you eat garbage, you feel garbage. Curate the input intentionally.

- The "Political" Mute: If someone treats LinkedIn like Twitter, mute.
- The "Humblebrag" Mute: If someone posts constantly about their own success to make you feel behind, mute.
- The "Doom" Mute: If someone shares constant catastrophic news, mute.

You are not being mean. You are protecting your cognitive environment. A curated feed should be boring or educational. It should never be emotional.

The Finite Media Diet

The problem with social media is that it is Infinite. You can scroll forever and never reach the end. The solution is to switch to Finite media.

The Strategy: Replace the Stream with the Bundle.

Stop getting your news from a timeline. Get it from a Newsletter or a Daily Briefing.

- Newsletters: They arrive once a day. They have a beginning and an end. When you finish reading, you are done.
- RSS Readers: (For the advanced). You choose the sources. You see the headlines. When the list is empty, you stop.

Shift your consumption from "Grazing" (random, constant

snacking on the feed) to "Dining" (sitting down for a specific, finite meal of information).

The "Browser-Only" Mobile Rule

If you must check social media on your phone, consider removing the app.

Force yourself to use the Mobile Browser.

- It is clunky.
- It is slow.
- It requires you to log in frequently.
- The interface is ugly.

This is the point. You want the experience to be bad. You want friction. The native App is a dopamine slot machine, polished to perfection. The mobile website is a utility. By making the experience slightly annoying, you break the trance. You will check it for 30 seconds instead of 30 minutes.

Strategic Reminder

The algorithm operates like a salesperson. Its goal is to keep you engaged. It is trying to sell your time to an advertiser. Every minute you save by blocking the feed is a minute you steal back for your own life. Limit the exposure.

Action: The Feed Training Protocol

Most people are passive.

When they see something they hate, a political rant, a gross video, a celebrity gossip trap, they just scroll past it. They roll their eyes and flick their thumb.

They think they are ignoring it.

They aren't.

By scrolling past it slowly, or pausing for a second to read the caption, you just told the algorithm: *"I am interested in this category, but maybe not this specific post."*

So it sends you more.

You have to stop scrolling and start voting.

You have a weapon. It is hidden behind three little dots in the corner of every post. It's called "Not Interested" (or "Don't Recommend Channel").

Start using it. Aggressively.

Treat your feed like a garden that has been overrun with weeds. You cannot just walk past the weeds and hope they die. You have to pull them out by the root.

The Protocol:

For the next three days, you are on patrol.

Every time you see a piece of content that doesn't serve your goals, every clickbait headline, every "rage-bait" video, every thirst trap, do not just scroll.

Stop. Click the dots. Tap "Not Interested."

It feels tedious. It takes two extra seconds. Do it anyway.

You are casting a negative vote. You are explicitly telling the machine, *"This is garbage. Remove it."*

If you do this ten times in a row, the algorithm panics. It realizes its model of you is wrong. It scrambles to find something else.

Then, you have to teach it what you do want.

When you see a video about science, or a post about history, or a beautiful piece of art, even if you don't have time to watch it right now, Like it.

Hit the heart. Save the post.

You are giving the dog a treat. You are saying, *"Yes. More of this. This is the signal."*

If you do this consistently for one week, your feed will change.

It will become quieter. It will become smarter. It will stop trying to trigger your reptile brain and start trying to serve your higher brain.

You will stop seeing the world as a chaotic mess, and start seeing it as a library you curated yourself.

Don't let them serve you the slop. Send it back to the kitchen.

CONCLUSION: THE QUIET MIND

Listen.

Do you hear that?

It's the sound of nothing.

Your phone is in the other room. It might be buzzing, or it might not be. You don't know.

And for the first time in a long time, you don't care.

That tightness in your chest, the phantom itch to reach into your pocket, to check, to scroll, to verify that the world is still there, it's gone.

You have reclaimed your brain.

When we started this, you were in the middle of a riot. Your attention was being pulled in a thousand directions by algorithms that are smarter than you and faster than you. You were bleeding out energy on things that didn't matter.

You were a host for other people's noise.

Now, the room is sterile.

The icons are gone. The notifications are silenced. The feed has been trained.

You didn't destroy the technology. You didn't move to a cabin in the woods. You just put the tools back in the toolbox. You closed the door.

This is what cognitive resources feel like when they aren't being looted.

It feels like boredom at first. Then it feels like space.

And then, finally, it feels like power.

You can sit with a single idea for twenty minutes without flinching. You can have a conversation with your spouse without looking over their shoulder. You can watch a movie without needing a second screen to keep you entertained.

You have stopped treating your life like a breaking news ticker.

You realized that most things aren't emergencies. They are just things. And they can wait.

This isn't just about productivity. It's not about getting more work done so you can make more money.

It's about dignity.

It is the basic human right to own your own thoughts. To decide what you care about, instead of having it decided for you by a server in California.

The noise will always be there. The world will always try to flood the hallway.

But you have a protocol now. You know how to triage.

You know how to stand in the middle of the chaos, completely still, and choose exactly what matters.

Welcome back.

FINAL CALL: THE DAILY PRACTICE

Don't kid yourself.

You are not "fixed."

This book isn't a vaccine. You don't take the shot once and walk away immune for the rest of your life.

That's not how focus works. That's not how the world works.

Tomorrow morning, the emails will come back. The group chats will light up. The news cycle will try to scare you. The algorithms will try to seduce you. Silicon Valley didn't turn off the servers just because you read a book.

They are still betting against you. And they have infinite patience.

If you stop the protocol, the noise will come back. It will seep in through the cracks, slowly at first, then all at once. You'll skip the Friday Flush. You'll leave the phone on the nightstand "just this once." You'll open a tab and forget to close it.

And a month from now, you'll be back in the waiting room, drowning in the flood.

Triage is not a destination.

It is a discipline.

It is something you have to do every single time you unlock a screen. You have to stand at the door of your own mind and ask the question:

"Is this vital? Or is this noise?"

Some days, you will fail. You will scroll for an hour. You will get sucked into a pointless argument. You will lose an afternoon to the drift.

That's fine.

Don't beat yourself up. Don't throw the system away because you had a bad Tuesday.

Just reset.

Close the tabs. Clear the desktop. Put the phone in the other room.

Begin again.

The goal isn't to be a robot that never gets distracted. The goal is to notice when you are drifting, and to have the tools to pull yourself back.

The emergency is over. The room is quiet.

Now, the real work begins.

Keep it sterile.

ABOUT THE AUTHOR

Marcus Thorne writes about cognitive clarity in a distracted age. His work explores how modern digital environments shape attention, behaviour, and decision-making, and how individuals can reclaim control without abandoning technology altogether.

Through structured frameworks and practical protocols, he focuses on helping professionals think more deliberately, work more strategically, and protect their mental resources in an increasingly algorithm-driven world.

The Dopamine Triage is the first instalment in The Cognitive Control Series, a collection of books dedicated to strengthening focus, discipline, and long-term intellectual resilience.

When he isn't writing, Marcus studies systems thinking, behavioural economics, and the evolving relationship between humans and technology.

THE COGNITIVE CONTROL SERIES

Book 1: The Dopamine Triage

Book 2: (Coming Soon)

---END---

9 789357 731188

Printed at Repro India Ltd.